904

Room 51

Dry Hill House

TONBRIDGE SCHOOL
ENGLISH DEPARTMENT

Frequencies

Verse by the same author

Song at the Year's Turning
Poetry for Supper
Tares
The Bread of Truth
Pietà
Not That He Brought Flowers
H'm
Selected Poems 1946–68
Laboratories of the Spirit

Frequencies

R. S. THOMAS

M

ISBN boards 0 333 23650 5
paper 0 333 23712 9

First published 1978 by
MACMILLAN LONDON LIMITED
4 Little Essex Street London WC2R 3LF
and Basingstoke
Associated companies in Delhi, Dublin,
Hong Kong, Johannesburg, Lagos, Melbourne,
New York, Singapore and Tokyo

Printed in Great Britain by
BUTLER & TANNER LIMITED
Frome and London

ENG
RS3S28K

CONTENTS

THE GAP

God woke, but the nightmare
did not recede. Word by word
the tower of speech grew.
He looked at it from the air
he reclined on. One word more and
it would be on a level
with him; vocabulary
would have triumphed. He
measured the thin gap
with his mind. No, no, no,
wider than that! But the nearness
persisted. How to live with
the fact, that was the feat
now. How to take his rest
on the edge of a chasm a
word could bridge.
              He leaned
over and looked in the dictionary
they used. There was the blank still
by his name of the same
order as the territory
between them, the verbal hunger
for the thing in itself. And the darkness
that is a god's blood swelled
in him, and he let it
to make the sign in the space
on the page, that is in all languages
and none; that is the grammarian's
torment and the mystery
at the cell's core, and the equation

that will not come out, and is
the narrowness that we stare
over into the eternal
silence that is the repose of God.

PRESENT

I engage with philosophy
in the morning, with the garden
in the afternoon. Evenings I
fish or coming home empty-handed
put on the music of
César Franck. It is enough,
this. I would be the mirror
of a mirror, effortlessly repeating
my reflections. But there is that
one who will not leave me
alone, writing to me
of her fear; and the news from the city
is not good. I am at the switchboard
of the exchanges of the people
of all time, receiving their messages
whether I will or no. Do you
love me? the voices cry.
And there is no answer; there are
only the treaties and take-overs,
and the vision of clasped
hands over the unquiet blood.

THE PORCH

Do you want to know his name?
It is forgotten. Would you learn
what he was like? He was like
anyone else, a man with ears
and eyes. Be it sufficient
that in a church porch on an evening
in winter, the moon rising, the frost
sharp, he was driven
to his knees and for no reason
he knew. The cold came at him;
his breath was carved angularly
as the tombstones; an owl screamed.

He had no power to pray.
His back turned on the interior
he looked out on a universe
that was without knowledge
of him and kept his place
there for an hour on that lean
threshold, neither outside nor in.

FISHING

Sometimes I go out with the small men
with dark faces and let my line
down quietly into the water, meditating
as they do for hours on end

on the nature and destiny of fish,
of how they are many and other and good
to eat, willing them by a sort of personal
magic to attach themselves to my hook.

The water is deep. Sometimes from far
down invisible messages arrive.
Often it seems it is for more than fish
that we seek; we wait for the

withheld answer to an insoluble
problem. Life is short. The sea starts
where the land ends; its surface
is all flowers, but within are the

grim inmates. The line trembles; mostly,
when we would reel in the catch, there
is nothing to see. The hook gleams, the
smooth face creases in an obscene

grin. But we fish on, and gradually
they accumulate, the bodies, in the torn
light that is about us and the air
echoes to their inaudible screaming.

GROPING

Moving away is only to the boundaries
of the self. Better to stay here,
I said, leaving the horizons
clear. The best journey to make
is inward. It is the interior
that calls. Eliot heard it.
Wordsworth turned from the great hills
of the north to the precipice
of his own mind, and let himself
down for the poetry stranded
on the bare ledges.
                        For some
it is all darkness; for me, too,
it is dark. But there are hands
there I can take, voices to hear
solider than the echoes
without. And sometimes a strange light
shines, purer than the moon,
casting no shadow, that is
the halo upon the bones
of the pioneers who died for truth.

IN CONTEXT

All my life I tried to believe
in the importance of what Thomas
should say now, do next.
                     There was a context
in which I lived; unseen forces
acted upon me, or made their adjustments
in turn. There was a larger pattern
we worked at: they on a big
loom, I with a small needle,
                         drawing the thread
through my mind, colouring it
with my own thought.
                  Yet a power guided
my hand. If an invisible company
waited to see what I would do,
I in my own way asked for
direction, so we should journey together
a little nearer the accomplishment
of the design.
                Impossible dreamer!
All those years the demolition
                     of the identity proceeded.
Fast as the cells constituted
themselves, they were replaced. It was not
I who lived, but life rather
that lived me. There was no developing
structure. There were only the changes
in the metabolism of a body
greater than mine, and the dismantling
by the self of a self it
                could not reassemble.

THE WOMAN

So beautiful – God himself quailed
at her approach: the long body curved
like the horizon. Why had he made
her so? How would it be, she said,
leaning towards him, if, instead of
quarrelling over it, we divided it
between us? You can have all the credit
for its invention, if you will leave the ordering
of it to me. He looked into her
eyes and saw far down the bones
of the generations that would navigate
by those great stars, but the pull of it
was too much. Yes, he thought, give me their minds'
tribute, and what they do with their bodies
is not my concern. He put his hand in his side
and drew out the thorn for the letting
of the ordained blood and touched her with
it. Go, he said. They shall come to you for ever
with their desire, and you shall bleed for them in
                                        return.

AT IT

I think he sits at that strange table
of Eddington's, that is not a table
at all, but nodes and molecules
pushing against molecules
and nodes; and he writes there
in invisible handwriting the instructions
the genes follow. I imagine his
face that is more the face
of a clock, and the time told by it
is now, though Greece is referred
to and Egypt and empires
not yet begun.
                And I would have
things to say to this God
at the judgement, storming at him,
as Job stormed, with the eloquence
of the abused heart. But there will be
no judgement other than the verdict
of his calculations, that abstruse
geometry that proceeds eternally
in the silence beyond right and wrong.

PLAY

Your move I would have
said, but he was not
playing; my game a dilemma
that was without horns.

As though one can sit at table
with God! His mind shines
on the black and the white
squares. We stake our all

on the capture of the one
queen, as though to hold life
to ransom. He, if he plays, plays
unconcernedly among the pawns.

That they should not advance
beyond certain limits left –
accidentally? – undefined;
and that compensation be paid
by the other side. Meanwhile the
peasant – There are no peasants
in Wales, he said, holding
his liquor as a gentleman
should not – went up and down
his acre, rejecting the pot
of gold at the rainbow's
end in favour of earthier
values: the subsidies gradually
propagating themselves on the guilt
of an urban class.
                              Strenuous
times! Never all day
did the procession of popular
images through the farm
kitchens cease; it was tiring
watching. Such truce as was
called in the invisible
warfare between bad and
worse was where two half-truths
faced one another over
the body of an exhausted
nation, each one waiting for
the other to be proved wrong.

NIGHT SKY

What they are saying is
that there is life there, too;
that the universe is the size it is
to enable us to catch up.

They have gone on from the human;
that shining is a reflection
of their intelligence. Godhead
is the colonisation by mind

of untenanted space. It is its own
light, a statement beyond language
of conceptual truth. Every night
is a rinsing myself of the darkness

that is in my veins. I let the stars inject me
with fire, silent as it is far,
but certain in its cauterising
of my despair. I am a slow

traveller, but there is more than time
to arrive. Resting in the intervals
of my breathing, I pick up the signals
relayed to me from a periphery I comprehend.

THE SMALL COUNTRY

Did I confuse the categories?
Was I blind?
Was I afraid of hubris
in identifying this land
with the kingdom? Those stories
about the far journeys, when it was here
at my door; the object
of my contempt that became
the toad with the jewel in its head!
Was a population so small
enough to be called, too many
to be chosen? I called it
an old man, ignoring the April
message proclaiming: Behold,
I make all things new.

The dinosaurs have gone their way
into the dark. The time-span
of their human counterparts
is shortened; everything
on this shrinking planet favours the survival
of the small people, whose horizons
are large only because they are content to look at them
from their own hills.
                I grow old,
bending to enter the promised
land that was here all the time,
happy to eat the bread that was baked
in the poets' oven, breaking my speech
from the perennial tree
of my people and holding it in my blind hand.

HENRY JAMES

It was the eloquence of the unsaid
thing, the nobility of the deed
not performed. They looked sideways
into each other's eyes, met casually
by intention. It was the significance
of an absence, the deprecation
of what was there, the failure
to prove anything that proved his point.

Richness is in the ability
of poverty to conceal itself.
After the curtains deliberately
kept drawn, his phrases were servants moving
silently about the great house of his prose
letting in sunlight into the empty rooms.

HESITATIONS

I rubbed it
and the spirit appeared
(of history): What you will,
it said. Die, I said.
But it would not.

Old gods are no good;
they are smaller than
they promise, or else they are large
like mountains, leaning over
the soul to admire themselves.

I put the bone back
in its place and went on
with my journey. History
went at my right side
hungry for the horizon.

Were there towns I came
to? The sky over
them was without expression.
No God there. I would have
passed on, but a music

detained me in one of
blood flowing, where two
people side by side
under the arc lamps
lay, from one to the other.

BRAVO!

Oh, I know it and don't
care. I know there is nothing in me
but cells and chromosomes
waiting to beget chromosomes
and cells. You could take me to pieces
and there would be no angel hard
by, wringing its hands over
the demolition of its temple.
I accept I'm predictable,
that of the thousands of choices
open to me the computer can calculate
the one I'll make. There is a woman
I know, who is the catalyst
of my conversions, who is
a mineral to dazzle. She will
grow old and her lovers will not
pardon her for it. I have made
her songs in the laboratory
of my understanding, explosives timed
to go off in the blandness of time's face.

PRE-CAMBRIAN

Here I think of the centuries,
six million of them, they say.
Yesterday a fine rain fell;
today the warmth has brought out the crowds.
After Christ, what? The molecules
are without redemption. My shadow
sunning itself on this stone
remembers the lava. Zeus looked down
on a brave world, but there was
no love there; the architecture
of their temples was less permanent
than these waves. Plato, Aristotle,
all those who furrowed the calmness
of their foreheads are responsible
for the bomb. I am charmed here
by the serenity of the reflections
in the sea's mirror. It is a window
as well. What I need
now is a faith to enable me to out-stare
the grinning faces of the inmates of its asylum,
the failed experiments God put away.

DIALECTIC

They spoke to him in Hebrew and he understood
them; in Latin and Italian and
he understood them. Speech palled
on them and they turned to the silence
of their equations. But God listened to them
as to a spider spinning its web
from its entrails, the mind swinging
to and fro over an abysm
of blankness. They are speaking to me still,
he decided, in the geometry
I delight in, in the figures
that beget more figures. I will answer
them as of old with the infinity
I feed on. If there were words once
they could not understand, I will show
them now space that is bounded
but without end, time that is where
they were or will be; the eternity
that is here for me and for them
there; the truth that with much labour
is born with them and is to be
sloughed off like some afterbirth of the spirit.

SHADOWS

I close my eyes.
The darkness implies your presence,
the shadow of your steep mind
on my world. I shiver in it.
It is not your light that
can blind us; it is the splendour
of your darkness.
                    And so I listen
instead and hear the language
of silence, the sentence
without an end. Is it I, then,
who am being addressed? A God's words
are for their own sake; we hear
at our peril. Many of us have gone
mad in the mastering
of your medium.
                    I will open
my eyes on a world where the problems
remain but our doctrines
protect us. The shadow of the bent cross
is warmer than yours. I see how the sinners
of history run in and out
at its dark doors and are not confounded.

Abercuawg! Where is it?
Where is Abercuawg, that
place where the cuckoos sing?
I asked the professors.
Lo, here, lo, there: on the banks
of a river they explained
how Cuawg had become Dulas.
There was the mansion, Dolguog,
not far off to confirm them. I
looked at the surface of the water,
but the place that I was seeking
was not reflected therein.
I looked as though through a clear
window at pebbles that were the ruins
of no building, with no birds tolling
among them, as in the towers of the mind.

An absence is how we become surer
of what we want. Abercuawg
is not here now, but there. And
there is the indefinable point,
the incarnation of a concept,
the moment at which a little
becomes a lot. I have listened
to the word 'Branwen' and pictured
the horses and the soil red
with their blood, and the trouble
in Ireland, and have opened
my eyes on a child, sticky
with sweets and snivel. And: 'Not

this,' I have cried. 'This is the name,
not the thing that the name
stands for.' I have no faith
that to put a name to
a thing is to bring it
before one. I am a seeker
in time for that which is
beyond time, that is everywhere
and nowhere; no more before
than after, yet always
about to be; whose duration is
of the mind, but free as
Bergson would say of the mind's
degradation of the eternal.

THE SIGNPOST

Casgob, it said, 2
miles. But I never went
there; left it like an ornament
on the mind's shelf, covered

with the dust of
its summers; a place on a diet
of the echoes of stopped
bells and children's

voices; white the architecture
of its clouds, stationary
its sunlight. It was best
so. I need a museum

for storing the dream's
brittler particles in. Time
is a main road, eternity
the turning that we don't take.

ADJUSTMENTS

Never known as anything
but an absence, I dare not name him
as God. Yet the adjustments
are made. There is an unseen
power, whose sphere is the cell
and the electron. We never catch
him at work, but can only say,
coming suddenly upon an amendment,
that here he has been. To demolish
a mountain you move it stone by stone
like the Japanese. To make a new coat
of an old, you add to it gradually
thread by thread, so such change
as occurs is more difficult to detect.

Patiently with invisible structures
he builds, and as patiently
we must pray, surrendering the ordering
of the ingredients to a wisdom that
is beyond our own. We must change the mood
to the passive. Let the deaf men
be helped; in the silence that has come
upon them, let some influence
work so those closed porches
be opened once more. Let the bomb
swerve. Let the raised knife of the murderer
be somehow deflected. There are no
laws there other than the limits of
our understanding. Remembering rock
penetrated by the grass-blade, corrected

by water, we must ask rather
for the transformation of the will
to evil, for more loving
mutations, for the better ventilating
of the atmosphere of the closed mind.

THE GAME

It is the play of a being
who is not serious in
his conclusions. Take this
from that, he says, and there is everything
left. Look over the edge
of the universe and you see
your own face staring
at you back, as it does
in a pool. And we are forced
into the game, reluctant
contestants; though the mathematicians
are best at it. Never mind, they
say, whether it is there
or not, so long as our like
can use it. And we are shattered
by their deductions. There is
a series that is without
end, yet the rules are built
on the impossibility of
its existence. It is
how you play, we cry, scanning
the future for an account
of our performance. But the rewards
are there even so, and history
festers with the numbers of the recipients
of them, the handsome, the fortunate,
the well-fed; those who cheated this
being when he was not looking.

WAITING

Face to face? Ah, no
God; such language falsifies
the relation. Nor side by side,
nor near you, nor anywhere
in time and space.
     Say you were,
when I came, your name
vouching for you, ubiquitous
in its explanations. The
earth bore and they reaped:
God, they said, looking
in your direction. The wind
changed; over the drowned
body it was you
they spat at.
     Young
I pronounced you. Older
I still do, but seldomer
now, leaning far out
over an immense depth, letting
your name go and waiting,
somewhere between faith and doubt,
for the echoes of its arrival.

THE POSSESSION

He is a religious man.
How often I have heard him say,
looking around him with his worried eyes
at the emptiness: There must be something.

It is the same at night, when,
rising from his fused prayers,
he faces the illuminated city
above him: All that brightness, he thinks,

and nobody there! I am nothing
religious. All I have is a piece
of the universal mind that reflects
infinite darkness between points of light.

GONE?

Will they say on some future
occasion, looking over the flogged acres
of ploughland: This was Prytherch country?
Nothing to show for it now: hedges
uprooted, walls gone, a mobile people
hurrying to and fro on their fast
tractors; a forest of aerials
as though an invading fleet invisibly
had come to anchor among these
financed hills. They copy the image
of themselves projected on their smooth
screens to the accompaniment of inane
music. They give grins and smiles
back in return for the money that is
spent on them. But where is the face
with the crazed eyes that through the unseen
drizzle of its tears looked out
on this land and found no beauty
in it, but accepted it, as a man
will who has needs in him that only
bare ground, black thorns and the sky's
                              emptiness can fulfil?

THE EMPTY CHURCH

They laid this stone trap
for him, enticing him with candles,
as though he would come like some huge moth
out of the darkness to beat there.
Ah, he had burned himself
before in the human flame
and escaped, leaving the reason
torn. He will not come any more

to our lure. Why, then, do I kneel still
striking my prayers on a stone
heart? Is it in hope one
of them will ignite yet and throw
on its illumined walls the shadow
of someone greater than I can understand?

ALBUM

My father is dead.
I who am look at him
who is not, as once he
went looking for me
in the woman who was.

There are pictures
of the two of them, no
need of a third, hand
in hand, hearts willing
to be one but not three.

What does it mean
life? I am here I am
there. Look! Suddenly
the young tool in their hands
for hurting one another.

And the camera says:
Smile; there is no wound
time gives that is not bandaged
by time. And so they do the
three of them at me who weep.

You are there also
at the foot of the precipice
of water that was too steep
for the drowned: their breath broke
and they fell. You have made an altar
out of the deck of the lost
trawler whose spars
are your cross. The sand crumbles
like bread; the wine is
the light quietly lying
in its own chalice. There is
a sacrament there more beauty
than terror whose ministrant
you are and the aisles are full
of the sea shapes coming to its celebration.

TRAVELS

I travelled, learned new ways
to deceive, smiling not
frowning; kept my lips supple
with lies; learned to digest
malice, knowing it tribute
to my success. Is the world
large? Are there areas uncharted
by the imagination? Never betray
your knowledge of them. Came here,
followed the river upward
to its beginning in the Welsh
moorland, prepared to analyse
its contents; stared at the smooth pupil
of water that stared at me
back as absent-mindedly as a god
in contemplation of his own
navel; felt the coldness
of unplumbed depths I should have
stayed here to fathom; watched the running
away of the resources
of water to form those far
seas that men must endeavour
to navigate on their voyage home.

PERHAPS

His intellect was the clear mirror
he looked in and saw the machinery of God
assemble itself? It was one that reflected
the emptiness that was where God
should have been. The mind's tools had
no power convincingly to put him
together. Looking in that mirror was a journey
through hill mist where, the higher
one ascends, the poorer the visibility
becomes. It could have led to despair
but for the consciousness of a presence
behind him, whose breath clouding
that looking-glass proved that it was alive.
To learn to distrust the distrust
of feeling – this then was the next step
for the seeker? To suffer himself to be persuaded
of intentions in being other than the crossing
of a receding boundary which did not exist?
To yield to an unfelt pressure that, irresistible
in itself, had the character of everything
but coercion? To believe, looking up
into invisible eyes shielded against love's
glare, in the ubiquity of a vast concern?

He had strange dreams
    that were real
in which he saw God
    showing him an aperture
      of the horizon wherein
    were flasks and test-tubes.
      And the rainbow
ended there not in a pot
    of gold, but in colours
that, dissected, had the ingredients of
    the death ray.

Faces at the window
    of his mind
had the false understanding
of flowers, but their eyes pointed
    like arrows to
    an imprisoning cell.
            Yet
he dreamed on in curves
    and equations
with the smell of saltpetre
in his nostrils, and saw the hole
    in God's side that is the wound
      of knowledge and
thrust his hand in it and believed.

EMERGING

Well, I said, better to wait
for him on some peninsula
of the spirit. Surely for one
with patience he will happen by
once in a while. It was the heart
spoke. The mind, sceptical as always
of the anthropomorphisms
of the fancy, knew he must be put together
like a poem or a composition
in music, that what he conforms to
is art. A promontory is a bare
place; no God leans down
out of the air to take the hand
extended to him. The generations have
watched there
in vain. We are beginning to see
now it is matter is the scaffolding
of spirit; that the poem emerges
from morphemes and phonemes; that
as form in sculpture is the prisoner
of the hard rock, so in everyday life
it is the plain facts and natural happenings
that conceal God and reveal him to us
little by little under the mind's tooling.

I am given to slum
clearance; I have thrown my images
outside where they accumulate
in a huge pile. It is not true
I am the house of prayer.
I am neither a voice
asking, nor is there an ear
that attends. If the best they can do
is to say I am the ghost
in the machine, I will lay
that ghost.
              The facts are
these: I live in a contemporary
dwelling in country that
is being consumed. Nature regards
me with a distrust that is
well-founded; there is no room
for us both. Small and compact
the house I occupy sustains
pressures as of the air's
fathoms, but I am not
at the bottom of them. I am
neither down here, nor
up there. I am where
I am, a being with no
view but out upon the uncertainties
of the imperatives of science.

AFTER JERICHO

There is an aggression of fact
to be resisted successfully
only in verse, that fights language
with its own tools. Smile, poet,

among the ruins of a vocabulary
you blew your trumpet against.
It was a conscript army; your words,
every one of them, are volunteers.

SYNOPSIS

Plato offered us little
the Aristotelians did not
take back. Later Spinoza
rationalised our approach;
we were taught that love
is an intellectual mode
of our being. Yet Hume questioned
the very existence of lover
or loved. The self he left us
with was what Kant
failed to transcend or Hegel
to dissolve: that grey subject
of dread that Søren Kierkegaard
depicted crossing its thousands
of fathoms; the beast that rages
through history; that presides smiling
at the councils of the positivists.

THE WHITE TIGER

It was beautiful as God
must be beautiful; glacial
eyes that had looked on
violence and come to terms

with it; a body too huge
and majestic for the cage in which
it had been put; up
and down in the shadow

of its own bulk it went,
lifting, as it turned,
the crumpled flower of its face
to look into my own

face without seeing me. It
was the colour of the moonlight
on snow and as quiet
as moonlight, but breathing

as you can imagine that
God breathes within the confines
of our definition of him, agonising
over immensities that will not return.

THE ANSWER

Not darkness but twilight
in which even the best
of minds must make its way
now. And slowly the questions
occur, vague but formidable
for all that. We pass our hands
over their surface like blind
men, feeling for the mechanism
that will swing them aside. They
yield, but only to re-form
as new problems; and one
does not even do that
but towers immovable
before us.
         Is there no way
other than thought of answering
its challenge? There is an anticipation
of it to the point of
dying. There have been times
when, after long on my knees
in a cold chancel, a stone has rolled
from my mind, and I have looked
in and seen the old questions lie
folded and in a place
by themselves, like the piled
graveclothes of love's risen body.

THE FILM OF GOD

Sound, too? The recorder
that picks up everything picked
up nothing but the natural
background. What language
does the god speak? And the camera's
lens, as sensitive to
an absence as to a presence,
saw what? What is the colour
of his thought?

               It was blank, then,
the screen, as far as he
was concerned? It was a bare
landscape and harsh, and geological
its time. But the rock was
bright, the illuminated manuscript
of the lichen. And a shadow,
as we watched, fell, as though
of an unseen writer bending over
his work.

               It was not cloud
because it was not cold,
and dark only from the candlepower
behind it. And we waited
for it to move, silently
as the spool turned, waited
for the figure that cast it
to come into view for us to
identify it, and it
didn't and we are still waiting.

THE ABSENCE

It is this great absence
that is like a presence, that compels
me to address it without hope
of a reply. It is a room I enter

from which someone has just
gone, the vestibule for the arrival
of one who has not yet come.
I modernise the anachronism

of my language, but he is no more here
than before. Genes and molecules
have no more power to call
him up than the incense of the Hebrews

at their altars. My equations fail
as my words do. What resource have I
other than the emptiness without him of my whole
being, a vacuum he may not abhor?

BALANCE

No piracy, but there is a plank
to walk over seventy thousand fathoms,
as Kierkegaard would say, and far out
from the land. I have abandoned
my theories, the easier certainties
of belief. There are no handrails to
grasp. I stand and on either side
there is the haggard gallery
of the dead, those who in their day
walked here and fell. Above and
beyond there is the galaxies'
violence, the meaningless wastage
of force, the chaos the blond
hero's leap over my head
brings him nearer to.
                              Is there a place
here for the spirit? Is there time
on this brief platform for anything
other than mind's failure to explain itself?

EPIPHANY

Three kings? Not even one
any more. Royalty
has gone to ground, its journeyings
over. Who now will bring

gifts and to what place? In
the manger there are only the toys
and the tinsel. The child
has become a man. Far

off from his cross in the wrong
season he sits at table
with us with on his head
the fool's cap of our paper money.

There is an island there is no going
to but in a small boat the way
the saints went, travelling the gallery
of the frightened faces of
the long-drowned, munching the gravel
of its beaches. So I have gone
up the salt lane to the building
with the stone altar and the candles
gone out, and kneeled and lifted
my eyes to the furious gargoyle
of the owl that is like a god
gone small and resentful. There
is no body in the stained window
of the sky now. Am I too late?
Were they too late also, those
first pilgrims? He is such a fast
God, always before us and
leaving as we arrive.

                        There are those here
not given to prayer, whose office
is the blank sea that they say daily.
What they listen to is not
hymns but the slow chemistry of the soil
that turns saints' bones to dust,
dust to an irritant of the nostril.

There is no time on this island.
The swinging pendulum of the tide
has no clock; the events
are dateless. These people are not

late or soon; they are just
here with only the one question
to ask, which life answers
by being in them. It is I
who ask. Was the pilgrimage
I made to come to my own
self, to learn that in times
like these and for one like me
God will never be plain and
out there, but dark rather and
inexplicable, as though he were in here?